7 STRATEGIES FOR ESTABLISHING A SUCCESSFUL BLENDED FAMILY

PRACTICAL GUIDANCE FOR COUPLES STRIVING FOR ONENESS WITHIN A BLENDED FAMILY

PASTOR MATTHEW JOHNSON

This publication is designed to provide experienced based authoritative information in regard to the subject matter covered. The publisher is not engaged in rendering psychological, financial, or legal service. It is sold with the understanding that if professional counseling assistance is needed in any area, it should be sought.

Scripture quotations taken from the King James Version.
Scripture quotations taken from the Amplified® Bible,
Copyright © 1954, 1958, 1962, 1964, 1965, 1987 by The Lockman
Foundation. Used by permission.

Scripture quotations are from the ESV® Bible (The Holy Bible, English Standard Version®), copyright © 2001 by Crossway, a publishing ministry of Good News Publishers. Used by permission. All rights reserved."

Womack House Publishing, LLC.
3965 East Brookstown Drive
Baton Rouge, LA 70805

www.womackhouse.com

Printed in the United States of America

ISBN 978-0-9904219-4-8 (pbk)

Library of Congress Cataloging-in-Publication Data applied for.

The publisher is not responsible for websites (or other content) that are not owned by the publisher.

The Womack House name and logo are trademarks of Womack House Publishing, LLC.

For information about special discounts for bulk purchases, speaking engagements or interviews contact Womack House Publishing via email at info@womackhouse.com or call 1-844-598-6654.

Contents

Introduction

For so long, there has existed a type of family unit that has not been adequately addressed within society's supportive circles. When we hear about topics concerning family, only one type of family unit seems to be touched upon, ignoring the critical need for specific guidance for the blended family unit, more commonly known as the stepfamily.

One doesn't have to examine the statistics to be aware that there is a desperate need for direction and advice, but for the sake of assessing this need, let's take a look at the numbers. A 2011 report by the Pew Research Center on adults in America updates our national statistics on stepfamilies for the first time in a decade. These statistics are on adults and do not include children, but they're staggering. Over 40% of adults have a step relationship—either a stepparent, a step or half sibling, or a stepchild.

You either know someone who is or you yourself are within a household of a blended family or step family, formed as the result of a remarriage with the biological parent of children who now live within the household. I decided to pen this book because of the astounding numbers mentioned above and to share my own personal experiences. People are hurting others, being hurt by others, and unknowingly tearing apart potentially successful relationships, and it's not because they do not love each other but rather because they lack a skillset and the personal awareness that they need in order to fulfill their roles properly.

Twenty-two years ago, it would have helped me tremendously to have had a book or even someone to sit down with me to give me some insight, strategies, and principles to turn to in establishing my blended family. This book's purpose is to give counsel and direction to those couples who are intending to bring two families together, as well as to assist couples who have already made the commitment.

I will address relationship dynamics, challenges, and issues that often arise within blended families in an effort to aid couples in creating the ultimate blended family unit they envision. It's my passion to support and educate new and existing families and give them guidelines that they can use in order to become one as a family.

We know that a proper foundation is the first component of any well-built structure. The family is much the same—its structure is built upon its foundation, the parents. They are the critical aspect to its success or failure.

Just to give you a little insight and history about my personal relationship—I knew of my wife long before we came into a marital relationship, or even a friendship with one another. It wasn't until years later that I saw her in a different light and desired a relationship with her, with the intention of marrying her at some point in time. The important thing that I did not consider was the responsibility of taking on a readymade family, without either the wisdom or experience to do so. My thinking, out of ignorance, of course, was that the children's mother and I would pursue a relationship with each other, and things would automatically flow from there. Actually, it was quite the contrary.

After we married, the reality of her having children quickly set in, and I started thinking, "What in the world have I gotten myself into? How will we make this work?" Even though I had no clue as to what I was doing in regards to the children, I still desired to be with my wife and become a part of the existing family. I saw what was missing, and that was the presence of a man in the house, and I wanted to fulfill that role.

Prior to this situation, without having this level of responsibility, it was very easy for me to say how much of a man I was, but it became apparent that taking responsibility for these individuals was much more than I had anticipated. I realized just how much work and attention would be required for this family to become all I envisioned it to be. So I dug in and went to work on myself, and I established my family. My desire is for your blended family to be what you envision, as well, and for you to gain the ability take the sensitive issues, challenges, and unique pitfalls head on and be victorious over them. Hopefully in some cases, you will be able to increase your awareness through preplanning so that your blended family may not have to encounter difficulties at all.

But first things first—assessing and addressing you, the parents, in working toward improving individually as well as together for the betterment of the family, both practically and spiritually.

Strategy 1
Establish Your Foundation

John 13:35 ESV proclaims,
"By this all people will know that you are my disciples, if you have love for one another."

Love for God
Love of Oneself
Love for your Mate
Love for your Family

In forming a blended family, the proper foundation—the parents—must come together in love about every aspect of the relationship and family.

To be of the correct mindset and heart, each individual must operate in and out of the love of God. That love, according to 1st Corinthians 12:4-7 ESV is patient and kind; it does not envy or boast; it is not arrogant or rude. It does not insist on its own way; it is not irritable or resentful; it does not rejoice at wrongdoing, but rejoices with the truth. Love bears all things, believes all things, hopes all things, and endures all things.

Even with the root force being the love of God—there are skillsets, habits, and thought processes that you will have to operate within in order to produce your desired results. The Bible specifically tells us that husbands should love their wives as Christ loved the church. That means that man's demonstration toward his wife should exemplify the love of Christ toward the church. Let's begin to look at some avenues in which you and your mate and family can work toward loving each other more.

In practicing love between each other, we must first get to know each other more.

Confession

Today we come together operating as one in and out of the love of God confessing that our lives are an endless loving expression to each other every day. In life as we grow stronger together in faith and love our family grows stronger as well. Our foundation is love and our love never fails.

We confess that our bond is sealed and our heart is set on a future that is bright, productive and rewarding all to the glory of God.

Key Points to Remember:

Strategy 2

Get to Know One Another

Don't be led by your emotions.

For those in new relationships or contemplating starting a blended family, the most common error I see is when individuals don't assess the situation properly before making a final decision. Most are allowing themselves to be led by their emotions.

The thing about emotions is they come and they go. They never stay the same, and this is simply because our emotions are dependent on circumstances and on how things are going at the moment. But this is where we often make crucial mistakes. We are governed by what we see, and there's nothing wrong with having some excitement—some emotions—about what we see, but when we allow ourselves to become governed or ruled by them, then we set ourselves up for failure and pain. In the end, we may discover that what we saw and what we have allowed ourselves to be governed or ruled by isn't what we really need for our lives.

A couple of relevant sayings that come to mind. The first— *Never judge a book by its cover*—and the second—*Just because it looks good doesn't necessarily mean that it is good.* Covers are designed to be appealing to the eye, to make one gravitate toward or be drawn to them. There's nothing wrong with being attracted to something or someone. But allowing ourselves to be overtaken by visual excitement without considering the situation in its entirety will later breed a place of frustration with the person we have connected ourselves to. Men are visual creatures, and we do not always take the time to step back and examine. I have to say that within the last ten years or so, women have increasingly been doing just the same as the men. Some women are becoming just as aggressive in nature, which is out of order in most cases. Order is essential, without it there will be chaos.

Emotions are powerful tools in the lives of individuals. They have the ability to powerfully affect how we function and operate in life. Emotions vacillate from day to day, and from moment to moment, simply because they are dependent upon the exterior circumstances around us that constantly feed them.

An emotionally ruled life is a life filled with pain, grief, and misery.

Situational

Billy, who has two children, met his beautiful wife, who has one child, two years ago. They married within two months of meeting. Within the first year, they were arguing constantly over just about everything—kids and money being the main issues. Billy assumed that because they had gotten along so well initially, they would never find themselves in a place of disharmony. They were both attracted to each other, and they had no problems with intimacy, but they neglected to discuss key family issues prior to getting married, and this left them miserable and filled with doubt about the future.

Advice for Billy

One key thing Billy could have done was take more time to get to know the woman he enjoyed—both through premarital counseling and in-depth discussions about relationship and family issues. These actions would have opened the door for both a dialogue and an education that could have potentially made the situation better for the couple as well as for the kids.

Key recommendations for potential blended families:

- Allot adequate time for a genuine friendship to develop between the couple, not just one of an intimate and sexual nature

11

- Non-biological parents need to spend time getting to know their potential spouse's children

- All individuals within the family need time with each other. Both sets of children must have adequate time to learn about each other.

  - Play dates depending on age of children
  - Family picnics
  - Game nights
  - Worship time
  - Dinner together
  - Daddy-daughter dates
  - Mother-son dates

Our emotions can camouflage what's real. They can disguise the reality of the kind of person one wants to become connected to, therefore causing us to miss out on the opportunity of discovering the *real* person we are attracted to. I don't want you to miss out on the kinds of moments that could be cherished for a lifetime. So take the time necessary to develop the relationships.

Confession: Getting to Know Your Mate

Father, today is the day we commit ourselves to knowing you and becoming intimately aware of who you are to us so that we can exemplify your love to our family. Ephesians 5:21 KJV states that we must "[submit] yourselves one to another in the fear of God."

We boldly confess that our communication is clear, and we are sensitive to each other's emotional needs. Today, we also commit our bodies to one another and honor our vows to you and to each other as husband and wife.

Key Points to Remember:

Strategy 3
Keep Your Commitment Strong

Proverbs 16:3 ESV states,
"Commit your work to the Lord,
and your plans will be established."

Commit to God
Commit to Yourself
Commit to Your Spouse
Commit to Your Family

For those within an existing marriage, one of the main issues you may face is how to remain committed to knowing one another. As previously stated, the essential ingredient in getting to know one another is spending quality time together. Quality, as defined by Webster, is *"a high level of value or excellence."*

Quality time has little to do with the *quantity* of the time you and your mate spend together. Quality beats quantity any day because of what it gives to each individual involved in the relationship. Figure out what works best for both you and your spouse. A planned date night once a week will have a tremendous impact on your relationship. The key is to keep in mind the best investment of your time. Quality time opens the lines of communication and gives you a true sense of a person's character and personality, establishing a bond on which to build trust.

Quality time brings a threefold intimacy of the mind, heart, and spirit, creating a sort of "wow factor", and this is where the true development of a relationship takes place. It gives you an opportunity to cater to each other's preferences, habits, and tendencies in a variety of situations. It helps both of you learn how to please one another. The wow factor encourages a good friendship, a satisfying love life, and a lifelong partnership that is bound by respect and honor for one another.

1 Peter 3:7 KJV states, "Likewise ye husbands, dwell with them according to knowledge, giving honor unto the wife, as unto the weaker vessel, and as being heirs together of the grace of life, that your prayers be not hindered."

I don't know a woman alive who would turn down focused quality time where she is given a chance to be honored outside the parameters of her normal day. A little goes a long way when opportunities are taken to concentrate on just the both of you.

Suggestions for making time for quality time:
- Date nights
- Weekend getaways
- Lunch dates
- Arrange for kids' time away from the home for private time
- Spend time to write out individual and family goals
- City sightseeing tours
- Support each other in activities and hobbies
- Special events and celebrations
- Working out together
- Wake up earlier and spend the first fifteen to thirty minutes of the day together

Beautiful friendships continue to develop over time, and this aids couples tremendously in enduring the challenges that are bound to occur, as well as potentially avoiding some. I encourage you to pray together, read relationship books based on your standards, study support material, and participate in activities that support vibrant relationships.

There will be obstacles, but obstacles were meant for overcomers to overcome!

Overcoming obstacles successfully within the relationship becomes a true testament of its fabric and adds to its depth.

The same mind and heart set applies to spending time with your family as a whole and children individually. Nurturing and caring for the children of a blended family is a necessary element, especially since children of these families have already been through experiences where their biological parents have separated or divorced. They are more likely to suffer with issues of abandonment and self-esteem depending on the circumstances they have encountered.

If you are the biological parent of the child, it is vital that you reassure them of your commitment to them and their wellbeing. For non-biological parents, being supportive, present, and available will reinforce your commitment to the children as well as reassure them of your commitment to their biological parent. These recommendations for newly blended families can also be applied to existing families.

Confession: Keeping Your Commitment Strong

Father, today I confess in the name of Jesus that our commitment to one another is strong and faithful. When making decisions, we consider each other's needs and love each other as Christ loves the church. We are fully committed to each other and speak against anything sent to divide us.

Today, let every word we speak to one another be faithful in order to display that we are safe with one another because our commitment is steadfast. We commit to loving one another with the love of God, and no weapon formed against us shall prosper.

Our commitment to each other never fails because it's rooted and grounded in Your love. Father, we thank You for your Holy Spirit guiding us within our relationship and ensuring that we remain in love and committed to each other in unity.

Key Points to Remember:

Strategy 4

Allow Man to be the Initiator

God wants us all to know and understand our assignments and then develop the God given abilities and acquired skillsets that will enable us to carry the assignments out successfully.

Today there is a trend that opens the door for significant issues to occur. Men are not acting as the initiator.

Which brings us to my next key for establishing your family. The male must be the initiator in establishing the pace and setting the tone and atmosphere of what the relationship should be like.

Women, Allow the Male to Be the Initiator

Many relationships have been functioning in the reverse, with the woman as the initiator of the relationship. She may therefore find herself being taken advantage of because she has become the giver and not the receiver. In many cases where the woman has been independent for a long period of time, this is a very difficult transition.

I believe this trend has contributed to men becoming lax in their position and in their responsibility for being the giver rather than the receiver. It is a critical error of our time.

Within Genesis, we see this principle represented when Adam gave names to every living creature, including woman. Man took the initiative. And so it has been—and always will be—the will of God that the man be the initiator of every area of life. It is the foundation on which everything was established, as well as the preferred pathway by which everything will be establish and built upon now and in the future.

This pattern was set into motion at the beginning of mankind. When it's reversed, the pattern, operation, and function of God's original plan is out of order. Without man, we have no woman and no mankind. Man is the seed giver, and woman is the receiver of that seed. The one who then gives birth to that which is sown. All of this allows the original plan of God to be fulfilled and divine order to take place.

Proverbs 18:22 KJV says, "Whoso findeth a wife findeth a good thing, and obtaineth favor of the Lord." This suggests that the woman—or the wife—has a big price tag attached to her. This is not to imply that she's money hungry or is a vain person, or that material things are her concern, but that the Creator has made her the greatest commodity that man can lay his hand on. She is far beyond rubies, as stated in Proverbs 31:19, but even better than that, there's *favor* that's connected with her, too, and the Lord's favor is more valuable than money could ever be.

Why Must the Man Be The Initiator Of The Relationship?

Why? Because he must be the one to reveal himself in a genuine way to the one he desires.

Key Ways in which Men Can Be Initiators

1. Initiating communication

Be willing to start sensitive conversations or break the ice and establish a line of communication.

*Coming together is one thing,
but staying together is another.*

Whatever the case, there will be legitimate questions and thought patterns that can be addressed for potential blended families as well as existing ones.

Questions that often come up for potential couples of blended families:

1. *Is this person the one for me?*

2. *Can I trust this person with my children?*

3. *Do I have what it takes to make this person happy?*

4. *Will our kids get along?*

5. *Will their kids like me?*

6. *How will my children react to the relationship?*

7. *Will my children respect my decision?*

Questions that often come up for both potential and existing blended families:

1. *How do we deal with children arguing amongst each other?*

2. *How do we come to agreements when non-biological parents have different viewpoints on subject matters?*

3. *What happens if one of the children is disrespectful toward a non-biological parent?*

4. *How do we ensure the kids feel they are being treated fairly?*

5. *How will we handle the other biological parents being involved in the children's lives?*

6. *Does my spouse really care for my children?*

7. *What will happen in case of a tragedy?*

It would greatly benefit the couple's relationship as well as the families for the male to initiate this often sensitive and important discussion.

2. Initiating vulnerability, transparency and honesty

Be willing to become vulnerable with your partner and children. With all the outside forces that kids encounter on a daily basis, this one is crucial. Most kids within blended families are open with the biological parent only and not the non-biological parent. This behavior, even though initially understandable, does not encourage overall family growth.

If you are the non-biological male parent, it's up to you to ensure that your non-biological children remain aware of your genuine interest and desire to be honest with them. This can usually be accomplished by sharing with them your commonalities and exhibiting behaviors that encourage them to trust you.

3. Initiating selfless acts

Always remember that what you demonstrate to your family will be either the rock or the quicksand of its existence.

Be willing to focus your attention on your partner and children, putting their needs, wants, and desires before your own.

The children and your spouse will take heed of all you do and say, both verbally and also in demonstration. They will remember it and, most times, emulate it. So if you desire a family of service-minded children, be of service and teach them what a service-oriented person looks like. Be yourself the first example of what it is you want them to be. The issues involving selfishness are so prevalent that I will discuss them in more detail later in the book.

4. Initiating assurance

Ensuring that your partner feels loved and important to you will bolster his/her confidence and aid him/her in living the best life possible. Your partner will be reassured within the heart as well as the mind that you genuinely value who they are to you, to your family, and to the world.

Married or single, young or old, every human has the emotional need to feel loved. When this need is met, we move out to reach our potential for God and our potential for good in the world. However, when we feel unloved, we struggle just to survive.

— Dr. Gary Chapman

Confession: He must be the initiator

Husband's Confession

Father, today is the day I commit myself to being the leader, father, husband, and man that you have created me to be. With this call and mandate upon my life, I commit to being and becoming the example our family should follow. I also make a commitment to open myself to acquiring the knowledge needed to become a good initiator for my family in every area, and that I may clearly and precisely communicate to my wife and children. In Jesus Name.

Suggested reading: Proverbs 3:6

Wife for Husband

Father, today I lift my husband up to you for insight and guidance to lead and love both myself and our children in the way you would have him do. I speak against anything and everything that attempts to hinder him from being the leader he was made to be. Today, I speak clarity and confidence into his life and spirit. In the matchless name of Jesus, Father, I thank you.

Key Points to Remember:

Strategy 5
Remain Open to Counsel

Proverbs 11:14 KJV states,
"Where no counsel is, the people fall:
but in the multitude of counsellers there is safety."

Families and martial relationships are failing at an alarming rate due to a lack of counsel. This is taking place within as well as outside of the church.

We must realize that it's alright—and important—to admit or acknowledge that we may not be knowledgeable about a particular subject or issue. It's even more important that when we find ourselves in that place, we seek advice from a creditable resource who is experienced in that particular subject matter.

A Pew Research study states that in 2013, four out of ten new marriages included at least one partner who had been married before.

Asking for help or assistance demonstrates that you are open to improvement for yourself and your marriage and are willing to do whatever is necessary to make the situation better. Proverbs 27:9 AMP states, "Oil and perfume rejoice the heart; so does the sweetness of a friend's counsel that comes from the heart." It's important when you seek counsel that the individual offers counsel according to the wisdom and the Word of God.

"He whose ear listens to the life-giving reproof will dwell among the wise. He who neglects discipline despises himself, But he who listens to reproof acquires understanding. The fear of the LORD is the instruction for wisdom, And before honor comes humility" (Proverbs 15:31-33, KJV). Once you receive instructions, follow through on that which is advised.

"Hear counsel, and receive instruction, that thou mayest be wise in thy latter end" (Proverbs 19:20, KJV). This gives you the golden keys to being wise in the time to come. It tells us we need to do three things—hear counsel, receive instruction, and accept correction.

Physically hear, mentally receive, and heartfully accept Godly correction and guidance.

A mindset of this nature positions you for success within any challenging situation.

"Only by pride cometh contention: but with the well advised is wisdom" (Proverbs 13:10-11, KJV). This is why marriage counseling is so important for your relationship. It is vital and will help you lay the proper foundation upon which your blended family can be successfully built. For existing blended families, it provides you with the wisdom you need to maneuver those inevitable bumps in the road.

With counseling, you will discover and uncover matters usually buried deep within the heart that hinder your ability to move forward in your life and relationships.

No individual comes with a manual. Two people coming together as one is complex due to their different backgrounds, personalities, and life experiences. But with proper counsel and God's direction, you and your family can overcome any and all challenges that you are confronted with and, at the same time, live up to your fullest potential.

Confession: Open to Counsel

Father, we declare that we are open to your counsel, for in your counsel is life and peace. We also understand that you have placed leaders in the areas of marriage and family to assist us in enhancing our relationships. We are open to receive and obey Godly instructions concerning our marriage and family so that our family may be blessed.

Suggested Reading: Proverbs 11:14

Key Points to Remember:

Strategy 6

Maintain a Mind Free of Selfishness

*Search me, O God, and know my heart! Try me and
know my thoughts! And see if there be any grievous way
in me, and lead me in the way everlasting!*

Psalm 139:23-24 ESV

*Do nothing from factional motives [through contentiousness, strife,
selfishness, or for unworthy ends] or prompted by conceit and empty
arrogance. Instead, in the true spirit of humility (lowliness of mind)
let each regard the others as better than and superior to himself
[thinking more highly of one another than you do of yourselves].*

Philippians 2:3 AMP

One of the biggest culprits—if not *the* root—of division and breakups within marriages and families is selfishness. Egotism, self-centeredness, excessive pride, arrogance, greed—all of these are traits and dispositions that no one, especially parents, should display. But yet they often rear their unattractive heads, doing so without regard for others who are affected greatly by them.

To obtain freedom from selfishness, you must first be able to identify or recognize what selfishness looks like. That means taking a good look at your tendencies, habits, conversations, and any other forms of communication both verbal and nonverbal.

We all at some point in time have been told "you're being selfish". The key is your response to those words. Do you stop to consider that there is a possibility that your actions demonstrate selfishness? Or do you choose to ignore it or shrug it off? Stopping to consider shows humility. An unwillingness to face it shows fear and arrogance. Shrugging it off is the easy thing to do, but owning up to it takes courage.

Set your heart to serve.

In creating your successful blended family, a humble mindset sets your heart to serve rather than to be served. "Even as the Son of Man came not to be served but to serve, and to give his life as a ransom for many" (Matthew 20:28

ESV). If every individual worked toward maintaining this mindset, success would be certain. It's especially important for parents to demonstrate selfless acts so that their children have a standard to follow within the home. If the children do not see you exemplifying selfless acts on a regular basis, you will be encouraging an attitude of selfishness, and it is this that they will display both inside and outside of the home.

Are you able to recognize when you are operating in a selfish manner?

Do you know what selfishness looks like?

Put simply, selfishness serves only one person—and that is *you*. Being a selfish person or individual puts you in the position of being and becoming a manipulator. This kind of person will always be seeking to have things their way, rather the way that's best for all involved.

Selfish motives and attitudes are very dangerous and hurtful to relationships. They don't allow the other person to be the receiver in the relationship, but always the giver.

Selfishness is your enemy—it stands in the way of you making genuine connections and achieving growing relationships. It will bring about a limited life versus the full prosperous one that you desire. God intended teamwork, partnership, and support in a relationship, but when selfishness surfaces, none of these can be achieved successfully.

Potential effects of selfishness within a blended family:

- Keeps you from sincere connections with non-biological children
- Eventually destroys any and all relationships of substance
- Keeps you and your family from reaching full potential
- Encourages selfish behavior in kids
- For men, it will hinder prayers

Remember 1 Peter 3:7 KJV states, "Likewise ye husbands, dwell with them according to knowledge, giving honor unto the wife, as unto the weaker vessel, and as being heirs together of the grace of life, that your prayers be not hindered." You cannot properly honor your wife or anyone else when operating in selfishness or with selfish intent.

The ugly deception of selfishness is that when operating in it, you usually feel as though you are on top or ahead. It's indeed a lie.

Operating in a selfish manner causes you to only think about yourself, which in turn denies anyone else in your care and consideration. The attention and focus is all on you—your wants, your needs, your desires.

Proverbs 14:12 KJV says, "There is a way which seemeth right unto a man, but the end thereof are the ways of death." So just because it may *seem* right doesn't necessarily means that it *is* right.

A selfish person looks at the gratification of the now, and they fail to look at the possibility of the end result.

If you find yourself struggling with selfishness—or maybe you just want to boost your level of service—here are a couple of things to try.

Practice Esteeming Others

Key word—practice. Just as a sports player practices for game day, so you should put time, energy, and concerted effort into practicing considering, appreciating, cherishing, and admiring others. It cannot be done passively, and for most will require attention to your thought processes and core way of thinking on a daily basis. For a wife, it could be something as simple as acknowledging your husband to the kids for cooking dinner. For a husband, it could be a simple compliment to your wife for all that she does on a daily basis for you and the kids.

Philippians 2:3 KJV says, "Let nothing be done through strife or vainglory; but in lowliness of mind let each esteem other better than themselves."

Become Faithful In Doing for the Other Person

Luke 16:12 AMP says, "And if you have not proved faithful in that which belongs to another (whether God or Man), who will give you that which is your own (that is, the true riches)?"

The idea is for you to become more involved in the needs of the other people—in this case, your family. Most times when we hear this scripture, it's used when individuals are speaking of being committed to church work outside of their home or supporting an individual in ministry. But proving yourself faithful to the needs of individuals within your home is just as important. Simple things like you making and keeping the commitment to take and pick up your spouse's dry cleaning every week. Even with all you can do or say for your mates and children, the most valuable gift you can give to them is a loving, wholehearted, dedicated YOU.

St. John 3:16 KJV says, "For God so loved the world, that He gave his only begotten Son, that whosoever believeth in him should not perish, but have everlasting life." He did not ask the world for a thing, and it's because He was already committed even before the fall of mankind, and they were then willing to recommit themselves to him. God is loving, and He gave His son to demonstrate His faithfulness and dedication to mankind.

Confession: How to Get Free of Selfishness

Today is the day you show us ourselves and reveal to us the areas in which we may be operating selfishly. We declare that we will not allow our hearts to be deceived by our emotions, and we will walk and operate in the truth of who we are and who God has intended us to be.

Key Points to Remember:

Strategy 7
Building Blocks for Securing Wholeness

Building Block #1
HONESTY

Proverbs 28:13 KJV says, "He that covereth his sins shall not prosper, but whoso confesseth and forsaketh them shall have mercy."

One of the most devastating things that could happen to a relationship is that a spouse finds out that their partner has been keeping a secret. Depending on the issue and the details, it could very well sever the bond that a couple has worked diligently to create. And it is for this reason that I suggest an open and honest relationship.

Secrets prevent individuals from experiencing the full potential of the power and blessings that lie within relationships.

Hiding anything about who you are—as well as your past—can have grave effects on your aim for a successful blended family.

I believe the number one reason why individuals choose to keep secrets is because of fear.

F – False (make it seem like the truth)

E - Evidence (it's certain that things have taken place)

A - Appear (it has been made to look as if it's true)

R - Real (it has become the vivid in your imagination)

Operating out of fear both hinders your progress and exposes trust issues. Even though it does take time to know your partner completely, it is fundamental that you make it a standard to not hide anything from one another. I'm not saying that you should give your life story and tell everything you've done in one sitting, but what I am saying is that when something does come up, and you realize you and your mate have not yet touched on it for whatever reason, you need to deal with it honestly and openly.

For newer couples still figuring out the ins and outs of your blended family, you may not be able to share everything within the first year or so, but you can maintain a mindset of honesty and truth with your significant other and family. There are things you have to face and accept—your partner had a life prior to you and may even have been married. There will be things that come up that they maybe just didn't think about mentioning. So don't blow up if you find out your spouse used to date one of your old friends from high school. Always remember 1 Corinthians:

Love is patient, love is kind. It does not envy, it does not boast, it is not proud. It does not dishonor others, it is not self-seeking, it is not easily angered, it keeps no record of wrongs. Love does not delight in evil but rejoices with the truth. It always protects, always trusts, always hopes, always perseveres. (1 Corinthians 13:4-7, NIV)

Fear paralyzes. It keeps you from your prospective future. Too often, we ascribe to the old saying, *what they don't know won't hurt them,* but the truth of the matter is, the things your spouse or family do not know have great potential to hurt them.

In addition to the withholding of secrets because of fear, I have witnessed individuals who decided to keep secrets for manipulative reasons and intentions. They chose to withhold information because of what they stood to gain—or lose. I see this with many couples, where one individual is benefitting more from the relationship than the other, selfishly taking all the benefits of being married without giving back the devotion and care the other person deserves and desires.

Considering all of this, I hope you can see the importance of honesty—both in the relationship with your spouse *and* with your family as a whole. Understand the possible detriment that can come from operating with manipulative, secretive, and hidden agendas—it can only lead to hurt, distrust, and disappointment. Just be honest.

Ways that we can work on this building block:

_____
_____
_____
_____
_____
_____
_____
_____
_____
_____
_____
_____
_____
_____
_____
_____
_____
_____
_____
_____
_____
_____

Building Block #2
COMMUNICATION

Seek to improve your communication skills. Isaiah 1:18, 19 KJV says, "Come now, and let us reason together, saith the Lord: though your sins be as scarlet, they shall be as white as snow; though they be red like crimson, they shall be as wool. If ye be willing and obedient, ye shall eat the good of the land..."

Did you know that more than half of the message you send when you're communicating is nonverbal? Eye contact, posture, expression, voice, gestures . . . all of these matter when communicating with your mate or family.

The ability to communicate effectively is yet another key component to the establishment and building of a successful blended family. Character, personality, and attitudes are revealed through communication. Maintaining a positive atmosphere within the home, resolving conflict, and practicing effective communication will give your family a sense of security and stability.

A good communicator is both a giver and a receiver—aiming to be clear about what he or she is saying and also able to receive the messages others convey. The act of communicating gives the recipient the opportunity to listen and know the heart of an individual. You receive what they are offering, whether good or bad. In resolving conflict, truth matters. To be an effective communicator, you must adhere to the truth and be diligent in addressing what's being said lovingly and productively.

The words *listen* and *hear* are not identical. Take a quick look at the following example.

Mary: John do you think we should go to the party tonight?

John: Mary, I thought I told you earlier I didn't think it was a good idea.

Mary: Oh yeah, I did hear you say that, I guess I forgot.

What happened with Mary is normal. She heard John, but she did not *listen* to what he was trying to communicate to her.

To hear someone means to perceive or apprehend sound by the ear. But listening means making a conscious choice to concentrate so that your brain can process what's being said. Too often, a person who is merely *hearing* is anxious to say something and, as a result, misses the opportunity to really listen and understand the point of the person speaking.

Adopting better communication skills will require shifts in habits and tendencies. In order to clearly hear and understand, one must be willing to listen more and speak less.

Hebrews 2:1 KJV says, "Therefore we ought to give the more earnest heed to the things which we have heard, lest at any time we should let them slip."

James 1:19-20 KJV says, "Wherefore, my beloved brethen, let every man be swift to hear, slow to speak, slow to wrath, For the wrath of man worketh not the righteousness of God."

This brings me to my last point for perfecting communication between couples and families, and that is an overall mindset to close the door on unnecessary family confusion that could occur during general conversations.

Close the door to family confusion by—

- Speaking to be understood, not to impress, instill fear, or demonstrate ego.

- Listening with full attention and having the intent to understand *what* is being said and not so much *how* it's being said.

- Avoiding emotional responses.

Ways that we can work on this building block:

_____
_____
_____
_____
_____
_____
_____
_____
_____
_____
_____
_____
_____
_____
_____
_____
_____
_____
_____
_____
_____
_____
_____

Building Block #3
VISION

If you fail to plan, you are planning to fail!
–Benjamin Franklin

Write and establish the vision you have for your family. For every aspect of our life, we should have a plan that will inspire and encourage us to keep reaching for the best in life and in ourselves.

Habakkuk 2:2,3 KJV says, "And the Lord answered me, and said, Write the vision, and make it plain upon tables, that he may run that readeth it. For the vision is yet for an appointed time, but at the end it shall speak, and not lie: though it tarry, wait for it; because it will surely come, it will not tarry."

Some even suggest using family mission statements. Stephen Covey states, "A family mission statement is a combined, unified expression from all family members of what your family is all about, what it is you really want to do and be, and the principles you choose to govern your family life."

Proverbs 29:18 KJV says, "Where there is no vision, the people perish: but he that keepeth the law, happy is he."

Developing a family vision or plan will aid in keeping you and your family motivated and moving forward. Even if you aim for the moon and only hit the treetops, it doesn't represent failure, it just means you have another day or a new opportunity to try again. So make a plan and work that plan together as a family—and eventually the plan will come to pass.

Ways that we can work on this building block:

_____

_____

_____

_____

_____

_____

_____

_____

_____

_____

_____

_____

_____

_____

_____

_____

_____

_____

_____

_____

_____

Building Block #4
TRUST

Develop and build your spouse and family.

This is a huge one. Below are five quick thought-provoking situations that address some of the main issues couples face in this area. For this exercise, you and your mate should answer the following questions individually. Assess where you are currently, and then work toward improving.

I check my mates' phone at least once a week.	Yes	No
I feel insecure when my mate is around attractive individuals.	Yes	No
I often think about whether my mate is cheating.	Yes	No
I dislike when my mate spends time with or around his/her ex.	Yes	No
I feel uneasy when my mate handles our finances.	Yes	No

If you answered *yes* to any of these questions, thank you for being honest. Please view this exercise as an opportunity for growth and development within your relationship. Work on the things that bother you and communicate effectively to your partner how you feel about them.

Remember that trust is something often developed through experience and time. Ensuring that you and your mate are on the same page about expectations and standards will foster the perfect atmosphere of trust for your family.

Ways that we can work
on this building block:

_____

_____

_____

_____

_____

_____

_____

_____

_____

_____

_____

_____

_____

_____

_____

_____

_____

_____

_____

_____

_____

_____

Confession: Honesty, Communication, Vision, and Trust

Honesty

Today, fear is no longer a factor in our lives nor in our relationship. We no longer assume what is or what may be, but we walk in the confidence of knowing that we are for each other and not against each other. Today, we declare that our past is behind us, and we move forward in faith fully trusting one another.

Communication

Today is the day we commit ourselves to becoming effective communicators. We listen to one another and praise, affirm, and respect each other. We are open to understanding each other's feelings, needs, and desires as we build a good foundation for our family.

Suggested readings: Hebrews 11:10, 2 Timothy 2:19

Vision

Lord, we come to you today in unity on behalf of the vision we have for our family. Today, we agree to stand on your Word and in your love for each family member. We speak against every assignment sent to hinder us and our fulfillment on this earth as your children and joint heirs with Christ Jesus. We trust you and your timing, Lord, and stand firm and patient.

Suggested readings: Habakkuk 2:3, Matthew 18:20

Trust

Today, we come together in love and in the agreement that we are committed to God, each other, and our family. We confirm our love through our words as well as our actions to establish and maintain the trust that we have for one another. Our bond is strong, and nothing can come between us because we are rooted and grounded in truth and love.

Challenging Questions
with Practical Advice

Challenge 1

We find ourselves constantly arguing when the kids are around, even though we know it will affect them negatively. Do you have any suggestions on how to handle these situations when the kids are around? We don't have a large home, so there's not much privacy.

Advice

1. One of you must not argue. It ceases to be an argument if only one person is doing the talking.

2. Somebody must be mature enough to take a moment and analyze the situation. Is the matter truly worth arguing over?

3. One partner must be mature enough to say we need to pick a later time and a different place in which to talk about the matter.

4. Somebody must ask the real question—what is this doing to our kids and our relationship?

5. The couple must take a look at themselves both individually and collectively and determine if this is the kind of example they want to be for their kids.

6. Perhaps consider counseling if none of the above options are working.

Challenge 2

Hello. My name is Wendy. We have a blended family with two children. The sixteen-year-old is my daughter from a previous marriage, and the thirteen-year-old is my husband's son from another marriage. I have found that our oldest child bullies our youngest. I would like to see her take on a more nurturing big sister role. How can we address the issue?

Advice

It sounds like the sixteen-year old isn't mature enough to take on such a role. It appears that she has some issues of her own that need to be dealt with first. So I suggest:

1. Both parents take a hands-on approach to helping the kids develop their relationship.

2. The mother of the sixteen-year-old should take the initiative to deal with her behavior. I think it's twofold—one of a selfish nature and of feeling her space has been invaded.

3. The husband must be given a greater voice in the life of the sixteen-year-old, if it hasn't already happened.

4. Find out why she's bullying the thirteen-year-old, then brainstorm solutions as to how the behavior can be changed.

5. Both parents must help the thirteen-year-old feel more secure about being a part of the family.

6. Watch for behavioral changes in the thirteen-year-old.

7. Have a family meeting of the minds by having an open dialogue with the kids.

Challenge 3

Hello, my name is Raquel, and I have recently married a man with two boys (ages eleven and fifteen) from two previous relationships. One of the mothers and I have a good relationship, but the other mother and I do not. The child from the mother that I do not get along with comes home constantly relating negative comments about me from his mother. How should we handle this situation?

Advice

Two separate entities as one unit—the mother and the child. All possible issues need to be explored, otherwise we can have unwanted situations arise that we don't want to have to deal with. So my suggestion is:

1. The parent of the child must deal with the child first of all.

2. The parent of the child must initiate and establish a rule of respect towards the parent figure.

3. The parent of the child should have a talk with the other parent concerning the negative remarks being repeated by the child.

4. The parent of the child should bring both the mother and his current wife together to see if he can bring about a solution to the problem.

5. If this persists/continues, then the father of the child will have to consider taking other meaningful steps to help the situation precautions before a wedge starts developing in the marriage.

Challenge 4

I recently married a woman, and I am finding we are having problems in the area of discipline. She prefers a more rigid and strict way of discipline, and I tend to be more lenient. How can we reach a common ground?

Advice

First of all, the disciplinarian should be determined before the marriage takes place, not after a situation begins to arise after marriage. This should have been a matter of discussion near the top of the list pre-marriage.

Second, the parent of the child/children should be the initiator of discipline of the child/children, but at the same time should find a way to involve the second parent figure so that he/she feels like they have a say in the life and rearing of the child/children. This establishes respect of the child/children toward the parent figure.

It's like having a tender hand with a firm grip. Even though my hand feels soft, my grip is firm. I'm refusing to allow things to get out of hand. The ideal is that I be willing to agree to disagree while still trying to develop and maintain an atmosphere conductive for growth and development within the family.

Both parents taking responsibility for the upbringing of the child/children will help with them become well-rounded and productive members in society.

Challenge 5

Hello, my name is Stacy. I come from a very giving family as opposed to my husband, who was raised in a more limited income family. We have had numerous disagreements about purchases for the kids—things like cell phones, electronic games, new shoes—all things that my husband deems as not necessary. I believe in rewarding my kids by giving gifts. What can we do to get on the same page?

Advice

There's a totally different perspective that comes from growing up in a financially comfortable family versus one that may not have been so stable in that area. And it's one thing to come from a giving family, and another thing completely to have been raised by a family that was not so giving—or maybe wasn't in a financial position to be giving.

There's nothing wrong with being in a position to be giving, but when it comes to establishing your own family with an individual coming from a totally different kind of background, you both must be willing to make some adjustments to avoid possible negative effects.

It is crucial to talk about issues of this kind before coming together in marriage. We don't want to enter into such an important union with the assumption that we can continue operating in exactly the same way as we did before getting married. If we do, we are setting ourselves up for disagreements or arguments about how money is being spent, driving a wedge between us. Money all of a sudden becomes an important factor in keeping a family a family, especially when a child/children are involved.

I don't believe in spending money on kids just because we have the means to do so. I believe that kids should be taught the responsibility of money and how valuable money can be when handled properly. So if money is going to be spent on the kids, there should be a consensus between the parents as to how and why a certain amount is being spent.

Suggestion:

1. Determine who handles the finances.

2. Determine how it will be spent.

3. Always allow your partner to know how it's being dispensed.

Establishing trust in every area of the relationship becomes key to keeping the family relationship intact.

Challenge 6

My name is Karl and I have been married to my wife for four years. We have three girls from previous relationships. I have noticed that my wife is particularly sarcastic to my daughters when I am not around. They have mentioned to me that my wife acts differently when I'm there. How can I assure my kids that they are safe and address my wife in this matter?

Advice

My hope is that you did not get readily upset about the matter because that could cloud your judgment. I would suggest the following:

1. You and your wife should sit down and talk about it between yourselves.

2. Be sure to approach your wife with a loving attitude, not one of judgment. I think you should approach the situation something like this—"Honey, can I talk

with you about something because I have a dilemma on my hands and in my heart." It must be dealt with in a way that won't appear that you have taken sides and have already decided she's at fault.

3. Then, after you have talked with your wife about the situation, you should bring everyone together and have family discussion about it to see if you can begin to build a relationship with the girls. It's obvious that something is going on between them, and you should take a look at how things started off before you decided to get married. Maybe you can recognize something that may have occurred then and deal with it from that perspective.

Challenge 7

My daughter has just turned sixteen, and I have told her that I will allow her to start dating. My husband thinks sixteen is too young. I want her to have the dating experience and have the ability to be open with me and not feel like she has to hide or sneak around.

Advice

You must first take a look at the fact that *you* made the decision, and *we* (you and your husband) didn't make the decision. In any situation like this, no single party should be making the final decision.

Next, if you want her to remain open with you, my question is *where does your husband fit into the equation?* It's understood that she isn't going to tell him the things that she will tell you, but at the same time, he must be given the privilege to have something to say in this matter. You must realize that you no longer have sole responsibility for the sixteen-year-old. He now has a level of responsibility and some say-so, so give him the privilege of sharing his insight from a male perspective.

I would tend to agree with him about the dating age because, more than likely, she's not mature enough to handle the responsibility of dating, which can and often will turn into a relationship of some sort. Until she becomes equipped with the necessary tools to function in dating and in developing a solid relationship, she should not be allowed to date.

Challenge 8

My husband and I have seven kids, four of which live four hours away. Every three months, he takes a trip to visit his kids, and I am not always invited to be a part of it due to my work. I am having trust issues. What should I do?

Advice

First of all, I would like you to determine whether or not your trust issues are valid. The trust issue you have with your husband— isn't because of a gut feeling, insecurity, or because he had done (or is doing something) that raises questions?

I think you need to talk with him honestly about your trust issue. One of the worst things you can do is assume what may not even exist. It becomes like a termite, slowly eating away at you, and that's when you will start becoming frustrated, disgusted, and even angry about the situation. You will be setting yourself up to create a situation with your husband that will be detrimental to your relationship.

Being able to talk becomes key to having and maintaining a good and healthy relationship with your partner. It's when you don't talk or refuse to talk that you will veer onto the path of losing what you have.

Challenge 9

I am currently contemplating a divorce from my wife because of her lack of love and support for my kids. She doesn't ask or inquire about them or attend any of their events. I did not see this before I married her. I am a firm believer in being there to show my kids my support? What should I do?

Advice

1. You and your wife should sit down talk about what caused her to change her behavior toward the kids.

2. Be open to what she has to say in regard to her relationship or lack of relationship with the kids.

3. Find out if she has a personal issue with you regarding the kids.

4. Think about whether or not you spend enough time with your wife in comparison to the kids.

5. Determine whether or not you are in tune with your wife's needs.

6. You must take responsibility for what's bothering you.

7. Pray about everything and don't settle for anything.

One of the most difficult things in establishing a blended family is being able to integrate another person into the lives of children. Children are not always accepting of someone who's not their biological parent. It takes a lot of work and wisdom to bring all parties together as one, so it's very important to add up those costs *before* marriage—and even before dating—to see if you are willing to put in the time, effort, and energy required.

Ten Key Scriptures to Keep Close

Let all bitterness and indignation and wrath (passion, rage, bad temper) and resentment (anger, animosity) and quarreling (brawling, clamor, contention) and slander (evil-speaking, abusive or blasphemous language) be banished from you, with all malice (spite, ill will, or baseness of any kind). And become useful and helpful and kind to one another, tenderhearted (compassionate, understanding, loving-hearted), forgiving one another [readily and freely], as God in Christ forgave you. (Ephesians 4:31-32, AMP)

Anxiety in a man's heart weighs him down, but a good word makes him glad. (Proverbs 12:25, ESV)

And let us consider one another to provoke unto love and to good works: Not forsaking the assembling of ourselves together, as the manner of some is; but exhorting one another: and so much the more, as ye see the day approaching. (Hebrews 10:24-25, KJV)

Pleasant words are as an honeycomb, sweet to the soul, and health to the bones. (Proverbs 16:24, KJV)

Wherefore comfort yourselves together, and edify one another, even as also ye do. (1 Thessalonians 5:11, KJV)

Casting down imaginations, and every high thing that exalteth itself against the knowledge of God, and bringing into captivity every thought to the obedience of Christ; (2 Corinthians 10:5, KJV)

And above all things have fervent charity among yourselves: for charity shall cover the multitude of sins. (1 Peter 4:8, KJV)

A soft answer turneth away wrath: but grievous words stir up anger. (Proverbs 15:1, KJV)

Brethren, if a man be overtaken in a fault, ye which are spiritual, restore such an one in the spirit of meekness; considering thyself, lest thou also be tempted. (Galatians 6:1, KJV)

Therefore confess your sins to each other and pray for each other so that you may be healed. The prayer of a righteous person is powerful and effective. (James 5:16, NIV)

About Pastor Matthew Johnson

Pastor Matthew Johnson is an author, speaker, and pastor of Faith Family Bible Church located in New Orleans, LA. He has been pastoring for twenty years and has been married for twenty-three years to his wife Diana L. Johnson. They are the proud parents of four children, and they have eighteen grandchildren and one great-grandchild.

Pastor Johnson's desire and purpose for writing this book is to help give counsel and direction to those couples who are intending to bring two separate families together into one unit. Because he didn't have anyone to sit down with him and give him insight as to how to manage the challenges of a blended family, he hopes that this book will give others seven strategies for establishing a successful blended family.

Made in the USA
Monee, IL
20 January 2022